Releasing The Spirit Into Your Flesh

Curry Blake

Copyright © 2019 by Curry R. Blake

All Rights Reserved

Published by

Christian Reality Books

P.O. Box 742947

Dallas, TX 75374

This book or parts thereof may not be reproduced in any form without express written permission of Curry Blake.

Printed in the United States of America.

"Learning to Live in Divine Health."

Curry Blake

www.jglm.org

At the time of this teaching we just returned from South Africa, even now we are still receiving testimonies. All my life I wanted to reach a place where I can see people get healed, see the power of God, see things happen and know that people are getting helped.

We receive more testimonies now than we ever have before.

What makes my heart jump the most is when I get testimonies from people like the one I was reading just before we came, that said, "Dear Brother Curry." Now, I don't know this person, I've never met them, they have not been in any of our meetings but they were from South Africa and they had heard what was going on there. At last count we had received documented reports of 300 people that are healed of AIDS, 300. I was only there 10 days. If I were able to stay there a month, we might be able to wipe that disease out of the whole continent.

We're getting these testimonies back and it is awesome getting testimonies like that, I've got to tell you, there's nothing like it, but... I get just as excited reading these other things where these people said, "I've been in healing ministry for over 21 years... hit and miss, seen some good things...but, this teaching just blows my mind" And they said, "We're going after it, we started applying what we've been learning and it's working."

As good as healings are, to get that report means something totally different. When a person gets healed they get healed, but when a person gets a hold of the gospel...the Message of God that works…it spreads.

A lady wrote me another testimony, she said she had this disease for 8 years. She kept asking God to heal her and doing everything she knew to do. She still couldn't get any peace or relief. At the conference we had a healing service and she wasn't in line, but she was going to get in line. She said, "You were praying for people and when you got down to the end they said 'come this way' and so you turned to walk off and I was standing there as you walked by," she said "you stopped, turned and took my hand and just said 'Be Blessed, it's going to be okay.' I went home that night, first night I've slept in 8 years, slept all the way through. When I woke up in the morning I was completely healed."

There's nothing like that.

But, I just want you to know, if you are even thinking about launching out in God. If it has even been a thought in your mind, maybe you think, "I would like to do something great for God, I would like to move out in God, I would like to touch lives, I want to help people." Let me encourage you, Do it! Is that simple enough?

Just do it! Don't wait!

"Well, but I've got to get more training, I've got to know more." Do that as you go, but don't wait. People are hurting, people are dying, waiting while you are learning. I'm not saying, "Don't learn." I'm just saying, "Don't wait to go. Learn as you go."

And if you do that, God will meet you wherever you are at, He'll meet you and it will grow. You just be consistent and keep doing it.

I want to take you to two places, first let's start in Philippians Chapter 3.

Now, tonight we're dealing with healing. If you preach the gospel you don't have to preach healing to get healing. If you preach healing, you'll get healing. But if you preach the gospel, you get healing. You don't have to preach healing to get healing. If you preach the Gospel, you'll get healing, but you don't have to preach healing to get healing.

Now, I'm going to preach on healing. I'm trying to get you out of the religious box that says, "It has to be this way, this is how God has to heal me, this is how God's going to do it."

The woman with the issue of blood said in herself, "If I touch the hem of His Garment, I'll be made whole," and that's what happened. She said the time for her healing. She said, "When I touch His hem, I'm going to get healed." Jesus didn't even know who touched Him, God didn't direct that healing, she directed it.

You can direct your healing. Do you know why you can do that? Because as far as God's concerned it's already done. He's already decreed it.

The biggest problem that I run across in Christian Circles is that we always think that God has to will our healing, or He has to flip the switch in heaven to get us healed and that He does it on a case by case situation. Or that He looks at you and says, "Yeah, you need healing... and to another and says "Umm, not right now" and I'm here to tell you, <u>God does not have to will your healing.</u>

Do you know why he doesn't have to will your healing? Because He has already willed your healing. It's called "Healing in the atonement". It was already paid for and purchased. Is healing in the atonement? Yes, it is. It is part of the Gospel; it is part of the price that Jesus paid.

I want to show you something. I'm going to try to get you beyond something. Moses said, that whenever God brought the people of Israel out of Egypt that He showed Israel His acts but to Moses God showed His ways.

Psalm 103:7, "He made known his ways unto Moses, his acts unto the children of Israel."

Do you remember when Moses was telling the people. I know you saw the miracles, but God showed me how He did them. You see that's better than seeing a miracle.

And that's exactly what Jesus was talking about with His own disciples in Matthew Chapter 14. Because at one point they came to Him and they said, "Lord, these people are hungry. Lord, you've got to send them away. They've got to go eat", and He said, "No, they don't have to go, you feed them." Now, that obviously caught their attention.

Back when Dr. Lake had his healing rooms up in Spokane a woman came to the healing room to be prayed for. She'd been prayed for several times, no result, nothing changed, so finally they came to him and said, "Brother Lake, this is what we're doing, and it doesn't seem to be working. We can't just get it to." And so he said, "Well, alright, I'll pray for her; I'll deal with her." So, they took her off to the side and he sat down next to her and he started talking to her and she said, "Yeah, I know, you know if you just lay hands and I know, yeah, and I know healing is in the atonement, yeah, I know." She already knew all the doctrine, she knew everything.

Do you understand? People that know the doctrine are usually the hardest people to get healed, because they already know it. It's like reading a scripture you've read a thousand times before. The next time you read it, you don't really read it, you just think, "Oh that, yeah" your mind runs forward to the end, because you've already heard it. That's the worst thing you can do, because you will miss the details that God wants to bring out for you right then. You should always look at the word of God as something precious and you want to look at each thing. It is like a jewel that you want to look at each facet of.

Lake himself even talked about a man that he trained under named John Alexander Dowie who was born in Scotland but was starting his ministry in Australia. He helped stop a plague or an epidemic that was killing his congregation. Whenever he saw this verse in the Book of Acts (10:38) that said, "how God anointed Jesus Christ of Nazareth with the Holy Ghost and with power, who went about doing good and healing all that were oppressed of the devil." He said up to that point he thought that God was the one bringing all this disease and gives all judgment. He said, "Then I realized, sickness is oppression from the Devil."

Do you know how he figured it out? Everybody in his church was dying, he heard that his piano player was in the throes of death right then. He was at his wits end of what to do and how to deal with it. So, he took his Bible and he walked over by the table and as he walked past it, he was very disgusted. Very depressed. And he threw his Bible. Just threw it on the table. And when he did, it fell open. And then he felt bad about how he treated the Bible. He went over there to close it and when he looked down, it was open at Acts 10:38. He read Acts 10:38 and he got it. And he realized, "Sickness is oppression. Sickness is not the will of God."

And then he said, he grabbed his hat, walked out the door, went down the road a little way to the house where the woman was dying, walked in and commanded that sickness to go because he knew it was from the devil and he said, as far as he was concerned, he was casting out a devil. Within a matter of minutes, the woman was well. Then he started going to the rest of his congregation and one by one they got well. That stopped the epidemic. Then shortly after that, he actually ran for a governmental position in Australia and lost terribly, which was the grace of God. If he had become a politician, he'd probably never have been a preacher. At least not to the degree that he was. Then he went to

America in 1888. Tremendous things happened and Dr. Lake went to train under him, because his family got healed under Dowie's ministry. And that was how Dr. Lake got started.

Now back to Dr. Lake. The woman that was there said, "Yeah. Everybody else has laid hands on me so just go ahead." And he said he stopped there for a moment and said, "You're a Christian?" She said, "Well, of course I am, sure I am." Then he said, "Well you have the Spirit of God in you?" She said, "Well, of course I do." He said, "Alright, I'm not going to pray for you. I'm not going to lay my hands on you. Here's what you're going to do. I want you to go over and sit in this chair. Are you saved?" And she said, "I've told you I'm saved." And he said, "So, Jesus lives in your Spirit?" And she said, "Yes." He said, "I want you to sit for a few minutes. I don't want you to do anything else. I'm not going to pray for you, and I don't want you to pray. I want you to just sit there and realize that as much as Jesus is in your Spirit. He wants to be in your soul and your flesh. And I want you to let Him out of your

Spirit, into your flesh." And she thought, "That's the most ridiculous thing I've ever heard."

But she sat there for a few minutes and started thinking about it. And he said, "Is Jesus in your flesh yet." And she said, "I don't understand what you're talking about." He waited a few moments. He said, "Just recognize, Jesus is in your Spirit. He wants out. Let Him out, just let Him into your flesh." A few more minutes, he said, "So where is Jesus? Have you let Him out yet?" and this woman looked at him and said, "He is in my flesh just like He is in my Spirit." And he said, "Yeah." She said, "No He's in my flesh. Just like He's in my Spirit." And she started getting more and more excited and started saying, "I've got it. I've got it; I understand He's in my Spirit and He's in my flesh!" And he looked at her and he said, "Well, if He is in your Spirit then death can't be in your Spirit." She said, "Well, of course not!" Lake said, "Well then, if He is in your flesh then death can't be in your flesh." She said, "That's right!" He said, "If death's not in your flesh then you can't get sick; you can't be sick." She said, "You're right. He's in my flesh and I'm healed."

She got up, healed.

Why? He didn't lay hands on her, she just recognized and let the Spirit that was in her spirit into her flesh. Now, do you realize what that means? That means that the Spirit of God in her the whole time was there to heal. The whole time.

Just like with the woman with the issue of blood. She was determining when Jesus healed. Only she thought, it was going to be some other way, because she had some other way in her mind, but whenever he showed her a way to get healed internally, that is when she was able to release the Spirit of God out of her Spirit and let the Spirit into her flesh.

You say, "I don't… I'm not sure I believe that." Then you don't believe scripture. Because the bible says, that if that same Spirit that raised Christ Jesus from the dead dwell in you, He will quicken, *make alive, heal,* your mortal body. Not your immortal body. Not your incorruptible body. Not your glorified body; your mortal body. The one you got right now. Do you see? Your glorified body won't need quickening. It's this body that needs it.

If you need healing, you don't have to wait till I lay hands on you. As a matter of fact, I really prefer that you don't. Because if you do then you're going to wait the next time I come around here. You are going to think something or say something and instead you're going to try to build up the fame of Curry Blake instead of the fame of Jesus.

If you can, just sit there and let the Spirit of God out of your Spirit. Quit containing Him and just let Him have free course in your flesh, then you can get healed while I'm talking. And that's even better. He wants you to let Him loose. Isn't that simple?

So, can I just ask you, is there anybody here that would say I do not have the Spirit of Christ in me? But if you don't have the Spirit of God, just raise your hand, say, "I do not have the Spirit of God dwelling in me", because the bible says, "If you have not the Spirit of Christ then you're none of his. So, what you're saying is you're not born again, you don't have Christ, you don't have the Spirit of God, you don't have the Spirit living in you. Is there anybody who does not have the Spirit of God living in you?

Okay, so I'm assuming everybody here has the Spirit of God. Let me ask you this. Will everybody that has the Spirit of God raise your hand? Well, that should be a hundred percent. So, if you all have the Spirit of God, then when we were worshiping just now, let me ask you this, were you really worshiping? Because worship, you know worship means to lick the hand. That's what it means, to lick the hand.

Okay, so in your own self whenever the music was going and the words were up and we're singing, is that what you were doing to God in the sense that you were just communing with him and just loving him? Is that what you were doing?

Okay, now, when you were doing that, let me ask you this, did you sense, not feel, but did you sense the Spirit of God? If you didn't, you weren't really worshiping. Because you really can't worship without sensing the Spirit. I'm not talking about goosebumps, that's feeling, but when you're communing with Him, there is a connection. When you connect with Him you sense Him. Don't make it weird, you are just in communion with Him.

If you sensed your communion with Him, the Bible calls it the communion of the Spirit, while we were worshipping, what caused that? What caused you to sense Him? Was it the music? Or was it the fact that you took a few moments to focus on Him? Not just you focusing on Him so that you can get something back. Let me tell you, if you're focusing on Him to get something back, then it is not pure worship. Pure worship is to lick the hand, not to have the hand stroke you. Okay?

So, if you were worshipping, then it was literally one sided, it really was, you were totally focused on giving out to Him. You were giving out love, devotion, everything of your being just toward Him. The beauty of that is, you can't do that without stirring Him up. And when you did that, that's what you sense. So, if you sensed Him, do you have to have the music to do that? You don't. We know it helps, its thank God for music. But at the same time, you don't have to have it to sense God. When we all focus on the same thing at the same time, it helps us all come into unity.

But individually, you could have walked out of here and walked down the hall and had the exact same thing, as long as you stayed focused on Him.

Let's do that for just a minute.

You say, "Curry, you almost had them, but now you broke the whole thing and now you're laughing saying; 'you can't do that'."

If that's true it is all psychological. You are to be able to switch from soul to Spirit that quick, (snipping) immediately. Why? Because its two different things.

While in church a few months ago, I noticed this child in worship and she is the perfect example of what I am talking about. We are all in here doing things, worshipping God, it's all awesome, it's good. She is laying on the floor. She was clapping her hands on the wood, keeping time with the music, but then she would just lay on the floor and roll around and just enjoying herself and that's what I am talking about.

Everyone thinks that you have to do everything just right, but I am just that kid sitting ono the floor having the time of my life. Everyone gets mad at me because I am in the way, but no one can say anything because my Daddy owns the company. That is what she reminds me of because she is just having a good time.

We were loving on Him and at the same time He was loving us. She was rolling around on the floor and He was loving her. At this point, she doesn't even recognize that there is a separation between her and God.

I'm not saying there is a separation, but that's what we think of. We think "I'm separated from God, now there's connection. I'm trying to connect, I want to connect, I'm worshipping you and I'm sure hoping you're receiving this." But she is just being her. She's not even thinking about, "Well, what am I supposed to be doing? I want God to love me, so I better do what everybody else is doing."

It wasn't in the physical thing of this that made God love you. That's the response to God loving you. What I am trying to get across to you is this: get to that point, where Jesus is your example, you are born again, you have the Spirit of God, and you recognize that, "I and my father are one."

Isn't it amazing? We always think, "I know Jesus and the Father are one but not too sure about me in the Father. Because there is this thing…" No, no, no! You were sin and now you've been made not righteous, but righteousness! You've been made righteousness. You've been made that. You were sin, but you are not any longer. Why? Because you were alienated from God, but you are not any longer, why? Because now you have been reconciled.

Do you know what reconcile means? We have different terminology, but when you reconcile your checkbook… you remember what it is to reconcile your checkbook, right? How do you know when it's reconciled? When it balances. What does that mean? Whenever the amount from the bank statement matches the amount in your checkbook. If it's a penny off it's not reconciled, if the numbers that are there differ from the numbers in your checkbook, it's not reconciled. The only time it's reconciled, is when both are identical. When there is no difference. You get it?

God put His Spirit in you, that's the part of you that's like Him. Your current physical body is not like Him, but in your spirit, you are like Him and there's one Spirit. He has made you just like Him in the Spirit, that means He's made you holy, He's made you sanctified, He's made you righteous, He's done all of that, He's given you His nature, His character, His Spirit, His name, His power, His work, etc.

Your balance and His books in Heaven match. There is no difference between them. The essence of all of this is Union, Union with Him. When you get a hold of that then you can look at somebody and instead of looking at them and saying, "Oh Father please, touch that one, and I'm laying hands to signify who I want You to heal." It's not that anymore, that's not how Jesus operated. Jesus looked at people and it says, "He took them by their hand" (Luke 8:54, Mark 9:27). Why? Because He was making that contact.

When Jesus grabbed them, God grabbed them. Well, I have news for you! When you grab them, God grabs them! Why? Because He is in you. He is not going to come down and touch them, He is going to come out and touch them. Now, notice, He didn't say, "I'll pour down my Spirit on you",

He said, "I'll pour out of my Spirit" Where is the Spirit? In you. You've got to move beyond you. You've got to get you off your mind and recognize what He did in you and who He created. This new creation, you've got to see that's what He created.

Do you see, if you say His words and you mean them and you're not just parroting them, but you really mean them, then whenever you speak His words, what did He say about His words? "My words are Spirit, and they are life."

Well guess what? Whenever I speak, if I'm speaking His words and I believed them, and I mean them, then whenever I speak, what am I doing? Then my words are Spirit. And they are life, why? Because they're the same word, the same Spirit is speaking them.

That's why you can reach down and take a child that is sick, and not have to say a word, just hold it. Reach down and just hug it and then hand it back to the parents and say, " The baby is going to be okay now." It's amazing because Christian parents get mad, "You didn't pray, I didn't hear you use the name of Jesus." Maybe I didn't. But I was doing it, in His name. As I hugged that child, life comes out, and death. whatever child whatever disease that child has, death has been swallowed up by life. Why? Because life is more powerful than death, it has already proven that. All you've got to do is, let that life flow out of your Spirit and into your flesh.

When you do that, it gets good and easy. You don't even have to think about half the stuff when it happens. Why? because He'll do exceedingly abundantly above all you can think or ask, according to the power that works in you.

Even before you call, He will answer.

See for most Christians, we can't fathom that, "Well, we've got to pray just right. How do I pray? I've got to do this." If He's going to answer before you call, the call really doesn't matter. How you call really doesn't matter; it's not a formula. Now, anybody can do this, any person with the Spirit of God, I don't care your age, I don't care, education has nothing to do with that. That's what they knew about the Apostles; they were ignorant and unlearned people. Right?

You are not to be brilliant. That's why Jesus could say, *"The Kingdom of God is at hand",* and then just set people free. Why? Because healing is evidence of The Kingdom of God. Why? Because in the Kingdom of God there is no sickness. He said, "I want to show you what it's like. Your will be done on earth as it is in Heaven."

So, what was He doing? He went about doing good healing everybody, why? No sick people in Heaven. He just went around trying to fix everything that was wrong and set people free.

That's all it was. The Kingdom of God is manifested like that. You just go about and do good. Set the people free, bring life and tell them, *"*Guess what, The Kingdom of God has come near to you.*"* You know? The way we would say in Texas is this, "This your lucky day." Why? Because help has arrived.

Let's go look at that scripture. I've got to read a scripture, so you won't think I'm not Christian.

Philippians 3:7

"But what things were gain to me, those I counted loss for Christ."

Everything that was good for me, everything that I had, I counted all loss for Christ.

Vs 8: *"Yea doubtless, and I count all things but loss for the Excellency of the knowledge of Christ Jesus."*

In other words, nothing matches that. Everything else pales to the knowledge of Jesus Christ.

Vs 8b: *"my Lord, for whom I have suffered the loss of all things, and do count them but dung, that I may win Christ."*

Vs 9: *"And be found in him, not having my own righteousness, which is of the law, but that which is through the faith of Christ, the righteousness which is of God by faith."*

How many of you have faith in Christ? Then you are righteous. Because that's how it comes, by faith in Christ. Not by your works, not by doing everything perfect. But, faith in Him that He took your sins and gave you His righteousness. It's not even your righteousness, it's His. I know this is fundamental.

Verse 10, that's where I want to get to. Why'd He care about dung, why'd He care about loss, why'd He give up everything?

Vs 10: *"That I may know him, and the power of His resurrection."*

Now, you notice he doesn't say, "And the power of His healing or the power of His miracles." Why? Because Paul said if Christ has not been raised from the dead then our faith is in vain. It was good that He hung on the cross. It was valuable for us, but what sets Christianity apart from everything is the Resurrection. Many religions have martyrs, but what makes Christianity different than all the rest is we don't have a martyr, we have a risen Lord. We have one whose resurrection broke the power of the enemy. When He hung on that tree, that's what He said, *"It is finished."* What did He mean? That people are free. Things are different, things have change.

In WWII, when we were in Okinawa, the battle was rough and went on for a period of time, many men died. Same thing with Iwo Jima and several of the other islands. It was amazing because even after they had planted the flag, (Well, when you plant the flag, that's supposed to mean here we are and it's our island) but even after they did that, even after some of the Japanese had surrendered there were still pockets of resistance. There were still people hiding and as they would go about to do business there would be snipers, Japanese snipers, they would be shooting at them and wounding them and doing all these things. As a matter of fact, even as late as up in the 1970s, there was at least one Japanese sniper that was still on the island of Okinawa, still shooting at people, never heard that the war was over. <u>Thirty years later!</u> Well, let me tell you, that's a good soldier. Thirty years and not a word from head-quarters, but he kept on fighting.

Yet we have Christians that have to get a word from head-quarters every morning or they give up. You've got to realize; we've been given commands; maybe He'll talk to us again whenever we finish the last thing that He told us to do. Why would He tell you something else if you hadn't finished the last thing? Maybe it's time we just start doing what He said. Even though we won the war there were still pockets of resistance. I'm telling you when Jesus hung out His arms and said it is finished, the war was finished. There was still a mop up that had to be done. As far as everything is concerned, He still had to go to the grave, He had to go through 3 days and go back up and all that.

I'm telling you as far as God was concerned, as far as history was concerned, that was it. But, there's still a mop up, we're still in a fight, there's still resistances and our job is to find the enemy anywhere he resists and drive him out and put our foot in the back of his knee and shove it to ground so that he has to bow his knee to our King because every knee shall bow. Ours bow first but then the enemy has to bow.

That's what healing is about. It is a demonstration, that's why Jesus uses healing as a demonstration that the Kingdom of God was here; that it had arrived, that it had shown up. Why? Because it showed that God is more powerful than any of the enemy's power. That's what it's about. That's not just to show that Jesus is God or who He was or a Messiah or anything like that. Many times, He healed people and said, "Don't tell anybody." He wouldn't do it to *prove* who He was. He was doing that *because* of who He was.

Well, I have news for you. That same Spirit dwells in you. That's who you are. You are born again and by nature a deliverer. That's your job, to set the oppressed free wherever you see them. Notice what He is saying, "To know Him and the power of His resurrection." That's what Paul said. He said, "I have purposed to know nothing among you saved Jesus Christ and Him crucified." Why? Because before the resurrection was the crucifixion. He was bringing Him to that point, to where He said, "All I want to know is Him crucified." Why? Because when He was crucified it is finished. It's done.

Our problem is we keep trying to get God to do something He has already done. Even to get God to do something done you need to enforce what He has done. You need to be praying that same prayer, "Your Kingdom come; Your will be done, on earth as it is in Heaven." Then remember that prayer and believe in the answers, then step out and fulfill it. Have you realized that Jesus purposely fulfilled scripture? Purposely, it says, "He healed them all", in Matthew chapter 8 verse 16. Why did He "Heal them all?" That it might be fulfilled that which is spoken by the prophet Isaiah.

You need a purpose to fulfill some prescriptions. You need to purposely be a believer that lays hands on the sick and they recover. You need to purposely be a believer that speaks in other tongues and speaks mysteries to God, and mysteries to yourselves and in your Spirit edifying you. These are prophecies that somebody is going to fulfill.

Go to Matthew 14:13-21,

Vs 13: "When Jesus heard of it, he departed thence by ship into a desert place apart, and when the people had heard thereof, they followed Him on foot out of the cities."

Vs 14: "And Jesus went forth, and saw a great multitude, and was moved with compassion toward them, and he healed their sick."

You hear that? Moved with compassion He healed their sick. Compassion heals. By the Spirit of God, then it says in verse 15.

Vs 15: "And when it was evening, his disciples came to him, saying, "This is a desert place, and the time is now past; send the multitude away, that they may go into the villages, and buy themselves victuals."

Vs 16: "but Jesus said unto them, "they need not depart give ye them to eat".

Here are the disciples saying, "look there's a lot of people here. It's late. You've got to send them in; they've got to get some food." He said, "No, they don't have to depart. I'm sure the disciples said, "Well, what are we going to do?" "They have to depart! We can't feed them!" That was their attitude, because they say unto Him,

Vs 17: "We have here but five loaves and two fishes."

Vs 18: "He said bring them hither to me."

Vs 19:"And he commanded the multitude to sit down on the grass and took the five loaves and two fishes and looking up to heaven He blessed and broke and gave the loaves to his disciples, and the disciples to the multitude."

Now, you'll notice, especially if you read in the other gospels too, the multiplication of the food did not happen in the hands of Jesus. It happened in the hands of the disciples. He said, "Bring it to me", He took it, He blessed it. Whenever they started handing it out is when it was multiplied. Through the other gospels you'll see that. We always want Jesus to do it, but Jesus is always saying you feed them. You do it. Put it in your hands. I have news for you, Jesus isn't here in the flesh anymore. He said He had to go because it'd be better for us if He did.

He's gone and it's better for us. Why? Because He sent back His Spirit to us so that we could do the work that He could do and greater works. Why greater works? Because we're facing a defeated foe. He faced a foe that was in full power at the time. It's easier for us, we should run faster; we should do more. Why? Because our enemy is defeated. But the enemy keeps convincing people that he is powerful. He says, "Boo", and everybody runs. It's time to say, "Boo" back. Right? The devils are more scared of you, than you are of them. Matter of fact, when they talk you shouldn't shake. But when you say the name of Jesus it says they tremble.

It's time for you to start making some devils tremble, Amen?

Maybe, I need to come there (down into the audience). And I need to put you up here (on the platform). All standing up. And then I'll just stand there. Because as long as you sit there you think, "I'm just a face in the crowd I'm nobody. He is the speaker he is the one that can do it. He is the special person He is the anointed person; He is…"

NO! I'm the trainer. Fivefold ministry, I'm to train and to equip. To grow you up into the image of Jesus Christ, to help you conform to that image. I'm a drill instructor, that means you've got to go to the battlefield. You are not just some face in the crowd, you're the soldiers; you've got to do the job, you feed them, you heal them, you set them free.

Knowing that the Spirit of Christ, that did it before, is in you now, that same Spirit that did it before is it any less Spirit?

Is He, is He lessened because He's in you?

He can't be, because He said it's better for us if He goes, because now we can do greater works. He can't be lessened in you. Jesus never intended His body, any individual member of his body to do less, than the original body did. You've got to realize this is who you are. This is your job. You are deliverers. There are people waiting for you to show up.

The Bible says, that there are people out there that are good works, that you have been created to walk in. That means when you walk past someone that is sick, hurting, crying or depressed or anything like that, and you walk right past them, you just walked past one of your good works. You should've stopped and said, "Here let me help you."

You say, "But I can't help them." No, don't even say that. Smith Wigglesworth said, "The person that has the 'I can' in him should never say I can't." Amen? this is who you are.

Now watch. He said here

Vs 20: "and they did eat and were filled, and they took out the fragments that remain twelve baskets full".

Vs 21: "And they that had eaten were about five thousand men besides women and children."

Do you realize that there was even more left over! When you do good like that you'll have more. "Well I can't give them my last dollar." Then don't ever expect God to bring you more. You give your last dollar. They had to give that out and there was more leftover than they started with. It's amazing how God does that. You help somebody and you'll have more left over than when you started. Now I'm not saying, He's going to counterfeit money and put it in your pocket, I'm not saying that. But He will make sure that you have more than you started with. "How do you know that?" Because the Bible says if you give to the poor, you lend to the Lord, and He will repay. It is that Simple.

If you are sick, it's not right for you to be sick. That's a miscarriage of justice. Because Jesus already bore sickness for you. It's a fact; it's there. He paid for it; it's a done deal. Do you have any problem asking a person to get saved? Meaning do you have any hindrance, is there any little thing in you that says, "God might not save that person"? Is there anybody that God won't save? You say no. Why? Because Jesus paid for everybody. Right? You're basing the fact that anybody can get saved on the fact that Jesus bore their sins. Right? Who forgives all thine iniquities, who heals all thy diseases, is the same verse! If you have no hesitancy to share the Gospel believing that people can be saved, any person can be saved.

Healing is just as sure. They are identical. They were both paid for in the same incident so to speak. Now it's just time to get healed, Amen? It is always God's will. Whenever the leper asks Jesus, "Lord if you will. You can make me clean. You can heal me." And Jesus didn't even hesitate He said, "I will, be thou clean." And immediately the leper's leprosy was cleansed. He was made whole. Now think about that. He said, "If you will", that word *will* doesn't mean *if you'll do it*. You look at that word *will,* it's in Matthew chapter 8. You look at that word *will* and it doesn't mean I will do it; it means I'm wilt to do it. It is my will; it is my desire; my intense desire.

As a matter of fact, if you go and look what the word fully means, it means not only will I do it, not only do I desire to do it, <u>but it is who I am in my nature.</u>

That's saying that it means it's always His will. Why? Because that's His nature. Jesus healed because it was His nature. He didn't look at individual cases and go, "Yeah, My Father wants that one well, no, you'll wait next year." He didn't do that. It was His nature. *"He went about doing good, healing all."* Every time, He healed them all, He healed them *all*.

People say, "Yeah they probably deserved it," No! It says, "He healed all that had need of healing." That goes beyond somebody being right enough to get it. Amen?

So, we're going to begin to do this now. I want you to take a minute. Remember when we started, I told about letting the Spirit of Christ come out of your Spirit and into your flesh. It is fine to lay hands but, you can't take my hand with you into the streets. You've got to be able to get it to the people. You've got to be able to feed them. You've got to be able to touch them; you've got to be able to meet their need. And so, for you to meet their need, you first have to be able to get your needs met. You should be first partaker.

So, right now, I want to give you an opportunity to get healed through Jesus touching you, directly by Him coming out of your Spirit and touching your flesh. Can we just take a minute to do that?

I'm trying to grow you up, I'm trying to get you beyond the looking at somebody else, I want you to look to Him.

Close your eyes if you have illness, sickness or disease in your body. You said you're born again, so we know you have the Spirit of Christ, so right now, just take a moment and do exactly what you were doing before when you were worshipping Him, and you sensed that connection with your Spirit and His Spirit.

As you do that, just begin, not saying a word, you've got to be able to worship inside as well as outside. Just take a moment and begin to worship right now, just worship Him. I'm not saying you have to say a word, don't make a sound, but just in you. Your body is your own little prayer closet. And right now, just connect, just connect with Him. And do it for a minute, and begin to sense, not feel, sense. What you sensed when we were worshipping a while ago. Remember that and it's the same thing, and just begin to let His Spirit just, start to kind of leak out of your Spirit into your flesh. And just let it start to permeate out, just start to kind of ooze out of your Spirit, and just start to touch into your flesh.

And if you had a sickness or disease, if you had cancer, you had tumors, you had pain, you had disks that were broken or disks that were messed up, raptured or out of whack or whatever, or you had low blood pressure, high blood pressure, diabetes, you have all these things going on. Let's take it even further than that, instead of focusing on the disease for a minute, I want you to focus on Him. So right now, let that Spirit of Christ pour out of your Spirit, and your Spirit shaped just like your body, but let that Spirit of Christ ooze out of your Spirit, and ooze over into your lungs. And heal the lungs. Because that life goes in and just drives out sickness. And let that Spirit of Christ ooze out of your Spirit. And let Him just ooze into your heart. And heal that heart problem. Heal that high blood pressure. Let that circulatory system just return to normal and function correctly in Jesus name. Right now,

and just begin that even now, you can do sev
things at the same time, just begin to thank Hı
for that, and appreciate Him for your healing.
Just do that right now, just begin to let that life
just flow and give you that connection. Just
sense Him for a minute, and I'm telling you, if
you'll do this, even on a regular basis, you'll stay
well. And the presence of God, will get stronger
and stronger in you and right now it may take a
few minutes to actually sense the presence of
God. But if you do this pretty regular, all of a
sudden, man, you close your eyes, and all of a
sudden that presence will just show up. And the
amazing thing about it is you start to get lost in
it. You have to be careful. Don't do this and
operate heavy equipment. Alright? Because you
can't, you just get lost... You won't want to
come back.

Right now, as you're doing this the Spirit of God
is healing your body. He's going through you, His
life is coursing to your veins, it is coursing
through your blood, going through your body,
and even now, right now while you are doing

this, just thank Him. Show Him that you appreciate it, and just love Him.

We're always into worship, lets worship. The Father seeks those that worship Him in Spirit and in truth. This is worshiping in Spirit. It's not the only way, but it is a way. And you'll get to where you start praying and you won't want to come back. And praying gets so easy. You think, "Well, I can't pray for very long. I get tired." Not if you do this. Just let His Spirit. Now, even now, while you are sitting there, His Spirit flowing through you, now, just take one hand, and just put it on your body where you've had pain, or where you've had a problem. Just put it there. Why? Because you're just making that connection and you are letting, directing it.

Dr. Lake used to say, "Between power and faith, choose faith, because faith directs power." When you put your hand on your body or on another person's body, you're directing it. You're intently putting it somewhere, and letting life flow in. Just let that Spirit, just emanate from you, even right now. Just, right now, you don't have to look at anybody, there's people around you that need help. So right now, just let the Spirit of Christ emanate from you. Just let it emanate, just let it go out from you, and it'll stretch out from you, and it'll find the person that has sickness, and let it touch them and let life flow into them and set them free. And all you have to do is agree with it, just agree.

Prayer

"Every sickness, every disease, you are defeated in Jesus' name. You can't even stay on these bodies. You can't even stay. And you will go. In the name of Jesus. Right now, I set these people free. I don't care what disease; the name doesn't matter. The name of Jesus is above every name. The name of Jesus defeats everything else. I don't care what you have, I don't care how long you've had it, I don't care what the cause is, bottom line is, the answer is Jesus. His Spirit. Even now, in Jesus name. Right now, autism I break your power, you are a liar, you cannot stay, you will go. Diabetes, you will go. Pain, go. In Jesus' name, right now, and we're not going to just focus on the physical aspect, right now, there are hurts emotional, hurts, hurts in the heart, people done you wrong, different things, and you haven't known how to get the rid of it, right now I'm saying, RIGHT NOW by a conscious act, I want you to right now, don't have to say that loud necessarily, but I want you to consciously right now, decide I forgive them. Right then, that's when the healing took place. Right now, you're healed. We command that pain to go, we command these memories to be healed. No more! You are born for peace. Because the Kingdom of God, is not in meat or drink, but righteousness, peace, and joy in the Holy Ghost, stay in the Spirit. Don't come out of the Spirit. Don't come out into the carnal. Stay in the Spirit. Don't get in the soul, stay in the Spirit, walk in the Spirit, let that Spirit walk in you and through you. Let the Spirit of God talk in you, let Him talk to you and through you. Right now, right now, just purposely push away all that junk. And just know, right now, "I am free. In Jesus' name." Right now, we speak peace... Peace to every family, to every family that has a child, that has any type of problem whatsoever. I'm telling you now, "Your answer is here. Peace... Peace... In Jesus' name." You can have peace, because He set your child free, in Jesus' name. Don't have to worry about the money, won't need that, when your child is free, in Jesus' name. Father, we thank You, we praise You, we magnify You. You are the God of Heaven and earth. You are mighty, mighty in battle, You, have shown us Your strong arm. You have delivered us. Your name, has brought us out. By the blood of Your Son, we thank You, right now we give You praise and honor and glory. Because You are the Most High God. There is none like You, none beside You, there is none other. You are magnificent. You are mighty. You are great. In the name of Jesus, Father, we thank You, and Father, we magnify the name of Your Son, and we say that, there is no other name, given among men whereby they must be saved. There is no salvation, in the name of Mohammad. There is no salvation in the name of Buddha. There is no salvation in any other name, but the name of Jesus and the glory of the Lord. The glory of the name. The fame of the name of Jesus, will fill this earth. And people will see, that You are the only True God. In Jesus' name.

Father, we thank You and right now, let's just give Him a shout and a praise, in the name of Jesus. Hallelujah! Father, we thank You, we praise You, we bless You, we thank You, Father, I thank You for setting these people free, in Jesus' name. In Jesus' name. And it'll be this way and no other. We thank You and we praise You, in the name of Jesus. So be it, so be it, so be it.

Amen